Step-by-Step, Practical Recipes Party Foo

Delicious Appetizers

A variety of fantastic light bites and appetizers that are guaranteed to appeal to your guests.

Party Desserts

Whether for a dinner party, children's party or any special occasion, these treats are sure to impress.

FLAME TREE RECIPE BOOKS

FLAME TREE has been creating family-friendly, classic and beginner recipes for our bestselling cookbooks for over 20 years now. Our mission is to offer you a wide range of expert-tested dishes, while providing clear images of the final dish so that you can match it to your own results. We hope you enjoy this super selection of recipes – there are plenty more to try! Titles in this series include:

**Cupcakes • Slow Cooker • Curries
Soups & Starters • Baking & Breads
Cooking on a Budget • Winter Warmers
Party Cakes • Meat Eats • Party Food
Chocolate • Sweet Treats**

www.flametreepublishing.com

Sesame Prawn Toasts

INGREDIENTS

Serves 4

125 g/4 oz peeled cooked prawns

1 tbsp cornflour

2 spring onions, peeled and
   roughly chopped

2 tsp freshly grated root ginger

2 tsp dark soy sauce

pinch of Chinese five spice
   powder (optional)

1 small egg, beaten

salt and freshly ground black pepper

6 thin slices day-old white bread

40 g/1½ oz sesame seeds

vegetable oil for deep-frying

chilli sauce, to serve

HELPFUL HINT

The toasts can be prepared to the end of step 3 up to 12 hours in advance. Cover and chill in the refrigerator until needed. It is important to use bread that is a day or two old and not fresh bread. Make sure that the prawns are well-drained before puréeing – pat them dry on absorbent kitchen paper, if necessary.

1 Place the prawns in a food processor or blender with the cornflour, spring onions, ginger, soy sauce and Chinese five spice powder, if using. Blend to a fairly smooth paste. Spoon into a bowl and stir in the beaten egg. Season to taste with salt and pepper.

2 Cut the crusts off the bread. Spread the prawn paste in an even layer on one side of each slice. Sprinkle over the sesame seeds and press down lightly.

3 Cut each slice diagonally into four triangles. Place on a board and chill in the refrigerator for 30 minutes.

4 Pour sufficient oil into a heavy-based saucepan or deep-fat fryer so that it is one-third full. Heat until it reaches a temperature of 180°C/350°F. Cook the toasts in batches of five or six, carefully lowering them seeded-side down into the oil. Deep-fry for 2–3 minutes, or until lightly browned, then turn over and cook for 1 minute more.

5 Using a slotted spoon, lift out the toasts and drain on absorbent kitchen paper. Keep warm while frying the remaining toasts. Arrange on a warmed platter and serve immediately with some chilli sauce for dipping.

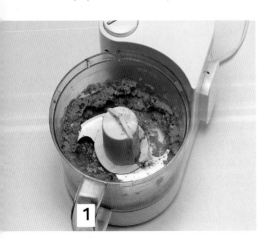

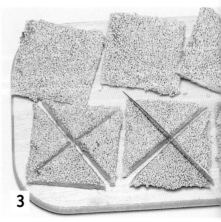

Fish Puff Tart

INGREDIENTS

Serves 4

350 g/12 oz prepared puff pastry,
  thawed if frozen
150 g/5 oz smoked haddock
150 g/5 oz cod
1 tbsp pesto sauce
2 tomatoes, sliced
125 g/4 oz goats' cheese, sliced
1 medium egg, beaten
freshly chopped parsley, to garnish

FOOD FACT

The Scottish name for smoked haddock is finnan haddie, named after the Scottish fishing village of Findon near Aberdeen. Smoked haddock has been a favourite breakfast dish in Findon and the rest of Scotland for many years. Although this type of fish was traditionally caught and smoked (sometimes over peat fires) in Scotland, nowadays the fish is produced in New England and other eastern coastal states of the United States.

1 Preheat the oven to 220°C/425°F/Gas Mark 7. On a lightly floured surface roll out the pastry into a 20.5 x 25.5 cm/8 x 10 inch rectangle.

2 Draw a 18 x 23 cm/7 x 9 inch rectangle in the centre of the pastry, to form a 2.5 cm/1 inch border. Be careful not to cut through the pastry.

3 Lightly cut criss-cross patterns in the border of the pastry with a knife.

4 Place the fish on a chopping board and with a sharp knife skin the cod and smoked haddock. Cut into thin slices.

5 Spread the pesto evenly over the bottom of the pastry case with the back of a spoon.

6 Arrange the fish, tomatoes and cheese in the pastry case and brush the pastry with the beaten egg.

7 Bake the tart in the preheated oven for 20–25 minutes, until the pastry is well risen, puffed and golden brown. Garnish with the chopped parsley and serve immediately.

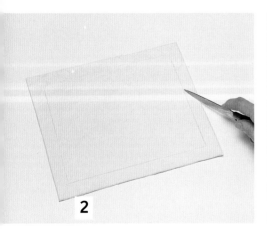

2

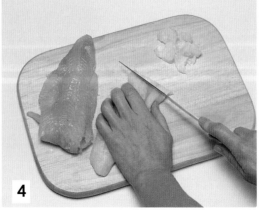

4

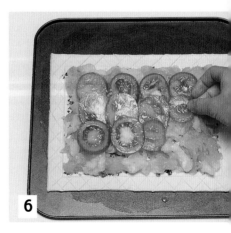

6

Smoked Mackerel Vol-au-Vents

INGREDIENTS

Serves 4

350 g/12 oz prepared puff pastry
1 small egg, beaten
2 tsp sesame seeds
225 g/8 oz peppered smoked
  mackerel, skinned and chopped
5 cm/2 inch piece cucumber
4 tbsp soft cream cheese
2 tbsp cranberry sauce
1 tbsp freshly chopped dill
1 tbsp finely grated lemon rind
dill sprigs, to garnish
mixed salad leaves, to serve

FOOD FACT

Mackerel is a relatively cheap fish and one of the richest sources of minerals, oils and vitamins available. This dish is an affordable way to incorporate all these essential nutrients into your diet.

1   Preheat the oven to 230°C/450°F/Gas Mark 8. Roll the pastry out on a lightly floured surface and using a 9 cm/3½ inch fluted cutter cut out 12 rounds.

2   Using a 1 cm/½ inch cutter, mark a lid in the centre of each round.

3   Place on a damp baking sheet and brush the rounds with a little beaten egg.

4   Sprinkle the pastry with the sesame seeds and bake in the preheated oven for 10–12 minutes, or until golden brown and well risen.

5   Transfer the vol-au-vents to a chopping board and when cool enough to touch carefully remove the lids with a small sharp knife.

6   Scoop out any uncooked pastry from the inside of each vol-au-vent, then return to the oven for 5–8 minutes to dry out. Remove and allow to cool.

7   Flake the mackerel into small pieces and reserve. Peel the cucumber if desired, cut into very small dice and add to the mackerel.

8   Beat the soft cream cheese with the cranberry sauce, dill and lemon rind. Stir in the mackerel and cucumber and use to fill the vol-au-vents. Place the lids on top and garnish with dill sprigs.

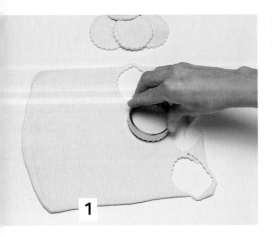

1

5

8

Dim Sum Pork Parcels

INGREDIENTS

Makes about 40

125 g/4 oz canned water chestnuts,
   drained and finely chopped
125 g/4 oz raw prawns, peeled,
   deveined and coarsely chopped
350 g/12 oz fresh pork mince
2 tbsp smoked bacon, finely chopped
1 tbsp light soy sauce, plus extra,
   to serve
1 tsp dark soy sauce
1 tbsp Chinese rice wine
2 tbsp fresh root ginger, peeled
   and finely chopped
3 spring onions, trimmed and
   finely chopped
2 tsp sesame oil
1 medium egg white, lightly beaten
salt and freshly ground black pepper
2 tsp sugar
40 wonton skins, thawed if frozen
toasted sesame seeds, to garnish
soy sauce, to serve

1 Place the water chestnuts, prawns, pork mince and bacon in a bowl and mix together. Add the soy sauces, Chinese rice wine, ginger, chopped spring onion, sesame oil and egg white. Season to taste with salt and pepper, sprinkle in the sugar and mix the filling thoroughly.

2 Place a spoonful of filling in the centre of a wonton skin. Bring the sides up and press around the filling to make a basket shape. Flatten the base of the skin, so the wonton stands solid. The top should be wide open, exposing the filling.

3 Place the parcels on a heatproof plate, on a wire rack inside a wok or on the base of a muslin-lined bamboo steamer. Place over a wok, half-filled with boiling water, cover, then steam the parcels for about 20 minutes. Do this in two batches. Transfer to a warmed serving plate, sprinkle with toasted sesame seeds, drizzle with soy sauce and serve immediately.

Bacon, Mushroom & Cheese Puffs

INGREDIENTS

Serves 4

1 tbsp olive oil

225 g/8 oz field mushrooms, wiped
  and roughly chopped

225 g/8 oz rindless streaky bacon,
  roughly chopped

2 tbsp freshly chopped parsley

salt and freshly ground black pepper

350 g/12 oz ready-rolled puff pastry
  sheets, thawed if frozen

25 g/1 oz Emmenthal cheese, grated

1 medium egg, beaten

salad leaves such as rocket or
  watercress, to garnish

tomatoes, to serve

TASTY TIP

The Emmenthal cheese in this recipe can be substituted for any other cheese, but for best results use a cheese such as Cheddar, which like Emmenthal melts easily. The bacon can also be substituted for slices of sweeter cured hams such as pancetta, speck, Parma or prosciutto.

1 Preheat the oven to 200°C/400°F/Gas Mark 6. Heat the olive oil in a large frying pan.

2 Add the mushrooms and bacon and fry for 6–8 minutes until golden in colour. Stir in the parsley, season to taste with salt and pepper and allow to cool.

3 Roll the sheet of pastry a little thinner on a lightly floured surface to a 30.5 cm/12 inch square. Cut the pastry into four equal squares.

4 Stir the grated Emmenthal cheese into the mushroom mixture. Spoon a quarter of the mixture on to one half of each square.

5 Brush the edges of the square with a little of the beaten egg.

6 Fold over the pastry to form a triangular parcel. Seal the edges well and place on a lightly oiled baking sheet. Repeat until the squares are done

7 Make shallow slashes in the top of the pastry with a knife.

8 Brush the parcels with the remaining beaten egg and cook in the preheated oven for 20 minutes, or until puffy and golden brown.

9 Serve warm or cold, garnished with the salad leaves and served with tomatoes.

2

4

7

Deep-fried Chicken Wings

INGREDIENTS

Serves 4

2 tsp turmeric
1 tsp hot chilli powder
1 tsp ground coriander
1 tsp ground cumin
3 garlic cloves, peeled and crushed
8 chicken wings
2 tbsp orange marmalade
2 tbsp ginger preserve or marmalade
1 tsp salt
3 tbsp rice wine vinegar
2 tbsp tomato ketchup
1 litre/1¾ pints vegetable oil for
   deep frying
lime wedges, to garnish

HELPFUL HINT

It is important to test the oil to make sure it is at the right temperature. If the oil is not hot enough, the chicken will be greasy but if it is too hot, the food may burn without being properly cooked through.

1 Blend the turmeric, chilli powder, ground coriander, ground cumin and garlic together in a small bowl. Dry the chicken wings thoroughly, using absorbent kitchen paper, then rub the spice mixture onto the skin of each chicken wing. Cover and chill in the refrigerator for at least 2 hours.

2 Meanwhile make the dipping sauce, by mixing together the marmalade, ginger preserve, salt, rice wine vinegar and tomato ketchup in a small saucepan. Heat until blended, leave to cool, then serve. If using straight away, spoon into a small dipping bowl, but if using later pour into a container with a close-fitting lid and store in the refrigerator.

3 Pour the oil into the wok and heat to 190°C/375°F, or until a small cube of bread dropped in the oil turns golden brown in 30 seconds. Cook two to three chicken wings at a time, lowering them into the hot oil, and frying for 3–4 minutes. Remove the wings, using a slotted spoon, and drain on absorbent kitchen paper. You may need to reheat the oil before cooking each batch.

4 When all the chicken wings are cooked, arrange on a warmed serving dish, garnish with the lime wedges and serve.

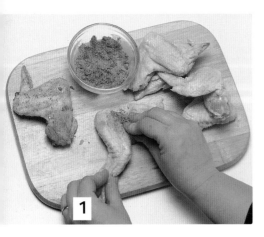

Chicken & Lamb Satay

INGREDIENTS

Makes 16

225 g/8 oz skinless, boneless chicken
225 g/8 oz lean lamb

For the marinade:
1 small onion, peeled and
   finely chopped
2 garlic cloves, peeled and crushed
2.5 cm/1 inch piece fresh root ginger,
   peeled and grated
4 tbsp soy sauce
1 tsp ground coriander
2 tsp dark brown sugar
2 tbsp lime juice
1 tbsp vegetable oil

For the peanut sauce:
300 ml/½ pint coconut milk
4 tbsp crunchy peanut butter
1 tbsp Thai fish sauce
1 tsp lime juice
1 tbsp chilli powder
1 tbsp brown sugar
salt and freshly ground black pepper

To garnish:
sprigs of fresh coriander
lime wedges

1 Preheat the grill just before cooking. Soak the bamboo skewers for 30 minutes before required. Cut the chicken and lamb into thin strips, about 7.5 cm/3 inches long and place in two shallow dishes. Blend all the marinade ingredients together, then pour half over the chicken and half over the lamb. Stir until lightly coated, then cover with clingfilm and leave to marinate in the refrigerator for at least 2 hours, turning occasionally.

2 Remove the chicken and lamb from the marinade and thread on to the skewers. Reserve the marinade. Cook under the preheated grill for 8–10 minutes or until cooked, turning and brushing with the marinade.

3 Meanwhile, make the peanut sauce. Blend the coconut milk with the peanut butter, fish sauce, lime juice, chilli powder and sugar. Pour into a saucepan and cook gently for 5 minutes, stirring occasionally, then season to taste with salt and pepper. Garnish with coriander sprigs and lime wedges and serve the satays with the prepared sauce.

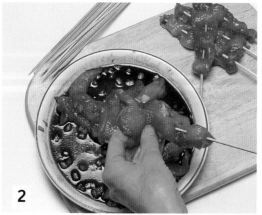

Vegetable Thai Spring Rolls

INGREDIENTS

Serves 4

50 g/2 oz cellophane vermicelli

4 dried shiitake mushrooms

1 tbsp groundnut oil

2 medium carrots, peeled and cut
into fine matchsticks

125 g/4 oz mangetout, cut
lengthways into fine strips

3 spring onions, trimmed
and chopped

125 g/4 oz canned bamboo shoots,
cut into fine matchsticks

1 cm/½ inch piece fresh root ginger,
peeled and grated

1 tbsp light soy sauce

1 medium egg, separated

salt and freshly ground black pepper

20 spring roll wrappers, each about
12.5 cm/5 inch square

vegetable oil for deep-frying

spring onion tassels, to garnish

1 Place the vermicelli in a bowl and pour over enough boiling water to cover. Leave to soak for 5 minutes or until softened, then drain. Cut into 7.5 cm/3 inch lengths. Soak the shiitake mushrooms in almost boiling water for 15 minutes, drain, discard the stalks and slice thinly.

2 Heat a wok or large frying pan, add the groundnut oil and when hot, add the carrots and stir-fry for 1 minute. Add the mangetout and spring onions and stir-fry for 2–3 minutes or until tender. Tip the vegetables into a bowl and leave to cool.

3 Stir the vermicelli and shiitake mushrooms into the cooled vegetables with the bamboo shoots, ginger, soy sauce and egg yolk. Season to taste with salt and pepper and mix thoroughly.

4 Brush the edges of a spring roll wrapper with a little beaten egg white. Spoon 2 teaspoons of the vegetable filling on to the wrapper, in a 7.5 cm/3 inch log shape 2.5 cm/1 inch from one edge. Fold the wrapper edge over the filling, then fold in the right and left sides. Brush the folded edges with more egg white and roll up neatly. Place on an oiled baking sheet, seam-side down and make the rest of the spring rolls.

5 Heat the oil in a heavy-based saucepan or deep-fat fryer to 180°C/350°F. Deep-fry the spring rolls, six at a time for 2–3 minutes, or until golden brown and crisp. Drain on absorbent kitchen paper and arrange on a warmed platter. Garnish with spring onion tassels and serve immediately.

1

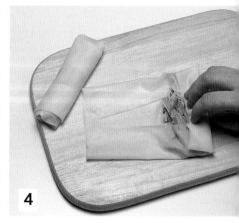

2

4

Potato Skins

INGREDIENTS

Serves 4

4 large baking potatoes
2 tbsp olive oil
2 tsp paprika
125 g/4 oz pancetta, roughly chopped
6 tbsp double cream
125 g/4 oz Gorgonzola cheese
1 tbsp freshly chopped parsley

To serve:
mayonnaise
sweet chilli dipping sauce
tossed green salad

FOOD FACT

A popular, well-known Italian cheese, Gorgonzola was first made over 1,100 years ago in the village of the same name near Milan. Now mostly produced in Lombardy, it is made from pasteurised cows' milk and allowed to ripen for at least 3 months, giving it a rich but not overpowering flavour. Unlike most blue cheeses, it should have a greater concentration of veining towards the centre of the cheese.

1 Preheat the oven to 200°C/400°F/Gas Mark 6. Scrub the potatoes, then prick a few times with a fork or skewer and place directly on the top shelf of the oven. Bake in the preheated oven for at least 1 hour, or until tender. The potatoes are cooked when they yield gently to the pressure of your hand.

2 Set the potatoes aside until cool enough to handle, then cut in half and scoop the flesh into a bowl and reserve. Preheat the grill and line the grill rack with tinfoil.

3 Mix together the oil and the paprika and use half to brush the outside of the potato skins. Place on the grill rack under the preheated hot grill and cook for 5 minutes, or until crisp, turning as necessary.

4 Heat the remaining paprika-flavoured oil and gently fry the pancetta until crisp. Add to the potato flesh along with the cream, Gorgonzola cheese and parsley. Halve the potato skins and fill with the Gorgonzola filling. Return to the oven for a further 15 minutes to heat through. Sprinkle with a little more paprika and serve immediately with mayonnaise, sweet chilli sauce and a green salad.

2

3

4

Sweet Potato Crisps with Mango Salsa

INGREDIENTS

Serves 6

For the salsa:

1 large mango, peeled, stoned and
  cut into small cubes
8 cherry tomatoes, quartered
½ cucumber, peeled if preferred and
  finely diced
1 red onion, peeled and finely chopped
pinch of sugar
1 red chilli, deseeded and
  finely chopped
2 tbsp rice vinegar
2 tbsp olive oil
grated rind and juice of 1 lime

450 g/1 lb sweet potatoes, peeled
  and thinly sliced
vegetable oil, for deep frying
sea salt
2 tbsp freshly chopped mint

1 To make the salsa, mix the mango with the tomatoes, cucumber and onion. Add the sugar, chilli, vinegar, oil and the lime rind and juice. Mix together thoroughly, cover and leave for 45–50 minutes.

2 Soak the potatoes in cold water for 40 minutes to remove as much of the excess starch as possible. Drain and dry thoroughly in a clean tea towel, or absorbent kitchen paper.

3 Heat the oil to 190°C/375°F in a deep fryer. When at the correct temperature, place half the potatoes in the frying basket, then carefully lower the potatoes into the hot oil and cook for 4–5 minutes, or until they are golden brown, shaking the basket every minute so that they do not stick together.

4 Drain the potato crisps on absorbent kitchen paper, sprinkle with sea salt and place under a preheated moderate grill for a few seconds to dry out. Repeat with the remaining potatoes. Stir the mint into the salsa and serve with the potato crisps.

1

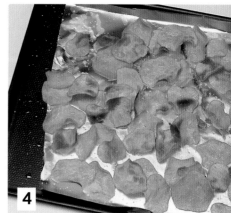
3

4

Three Tomato Pizza

INGREDIENTS

Serves 2–4

Basic pizza dough:

225 g/8 oz strong plain flour
1/2 tsp salt
1/4 tsp quick-acting dried yeast
150 ml/1/4 pint warm water
1 tbsp extra virgin olive oil

For the topping:

3 plum tomatoes
8 cherry tomatoes
6 sun-dried tomatoes
pinch of sea salt
1 tbsp freshly chopped basil
2 tbsp extra virgin olive oil
125 g/4 oz buffalo mozzarella
   cheese, sliced
freshly ground black pepper
fresh basil leaves, to garnish

1 Preheat the oven to 220°C/425°F/Gas Mark 7. Sift the flour and salt into a bowl and stir in the yeast. Make a well in the centre and gradually add the water and oil to form a soft dough. Knead the dough on a floured surface for about 5 minutes until smooth and elastic. Place in a lightly oiled bowl and cover with clingfilm. Leave to rise in a warm place for 1 hour.

2 Knock the pizza dough with your fist a few times, shape and roll out thinly on a lightly floured board. Place on a lightly floured baking sheet and lift the edge to make a little rim. Place a baking sheet into the oven to heat up.

3 Divide the pizza dough into four equal pieces. Roll out one piece on a lightly floured board to form a 20.5 cm/8 inch round. Lightly cover the three remaining pieces of dough with clingfilm.

4 Roll out the other three pieces into rounds, one at a time. While rolling out any piece of dough, keep the others covered with the clingfilm.

5 Slice the plum tomatoes, halve the cherry tomatoes and chop the sun-dried tomatoes into small pieces.

6 Place a few pieces of each type of tomato on each pizza base then season to taste with the sea salt.

7 Sprinkle with the chopped basil and drizzle with the olive oil. Place a few slices of mozzarella on each pizza and season with black pepper.

8 Transfer the pizza on to the heated baking sheet and cook for 15–20 minutes, or until the cheese is golden brown and bubbling. Garnish with the basil leaves and serve immediately.

3

6

7

Raspberry Chocolate Ganache & Berry Tartlets

INGREDIENTS

Serves 8

For the chocolate pastry:
125 g/4 oz unsalted butter, softened
60 g/2½ oz caster sugar
2 tsp vanilla essence
175 g/6 oz plain flour, sifted
40 g/1½ oz cocoa powder

For the filling:
600 ml/1 pint whipping cream
275 g/10 oz seedless raspberry jam
225 g/8 oz plain dark
   chocolate, chopped
700 g/1½ lb raspberries or other
   summer berries
50 ml/2 fl oz framboise liqueur
1 tbsp caster sugar
crème fraîche, to serve

TASTY TIP
Try substituting an equal quantity of white chocolate for the plain chocolate in this recipe, as raspberries go very well with it.

1 Preheat the oven to 200°C/400°F/Gas Mark 6, 15 minutes before cooking. Make the chocolate pastry by putting the butter, sugar and vanilla essence into a food processor and blending until creamy. Add the flour and cocoa powder and process until a soft dough forms. Wrap in clingfilm, chill for at least 1 hour, and then use to line eight 7.5 cm/3 inch tartlet tins. Bake blind in the preheated oven for 12 minutes.

2 Place 400 ml/14 fl oz of the cream and half of the raspberry jam in a saucepan and bring to the boil, whisking constantly to dissolve the jam. Remove from the heat and add the chocolate all at once, stirring until the chocolate has melted.

3 Pour into the pastry-lined tartlet tins, shaking gently to distribute the ganache evenly. Chill in the refrigerator for 1 hour or until set.

4 Place the berries in a large shallow bowl. Heat the remaining raspberry jam with half the framboise liqueur over a medium heat until melted and bubbling. Drizzle over the berries and toss gently to coat.

5 Divide the berries among the tartlets, piling them up if necessary. Chill in the refrigerator until ready to serve.

6 Remove the tartlets from the refrigerator for at least 30 minutes before serving. Using an electric whisk, whisk the remaining cream with the caster sugar and the remaining framboise liqueur until it is thick and softly peaking. Serve with the tartlets and crème fraîche.

1

2

3

White Chocolate Mousse & Strawberry Tart

INGREDIENTS

Cuts into 10 slices

1 quantity shop-bought sweet
   shortcrust pastry
60 g/2½ oz strawberry jam
1–2 tbsp kirsch or framboise liqueur
450–700 g/1–1½ lb ripe strawberries,
   sliced lengthways

For the white chocolate mousse:
250 g/9 oz white chocolate, chopped
350 ml/12 oz double cream
3 tbsp kirsch or framboise liqueur
1–2 large egg whites (optional)

HELPFUL HINT

This recipe contains raw egg whites, which should be eaten with caution by vulnerable groups including the elderly, young and pregnant women. If you are worried, omit them from the recipe.

1 Preheat the oven to 200°C/400°F/Gas Mark 6, 15 minutes before baking. Roll the prepared pastry out on a lightly floured surface and use to line a 25.5 cm/10 inch flan tin.

2 Line with either tinfoil or nonstick baking parchment and baking beans then bake blind in the preheated oven for 15–20 minutes. Remove the tinfoil or baking parchment and return to the oven for a further 5 minutes.

3 To make the mousse, place the white chocolate with 2 tablespoons of water and 125 ml/4 fl oz of the cream in a saucepan and heat gently, stirring until the chocolate has melted and is smooth. Remove from the heat, stir in the kirsch or framboise liqueur and cool.

4 Whip the remaining cream until soft peaks form. Fold a spoonful of the cream into the cooled white chocolate mixture, then fold in the remaining cream. If using, whisk the egg whites until stiff and gently fold into the white chocolate cream mixture to make a softer, lighter mousse. Chill in the refrigerator for 15–20 minutes.

5 Heat the strawberry jam with the kirsch or framboise liqueur and brush or spread half the mixture onto the pastry base. Leave to cool.

6 Spread the chilled chocolate mousse over the jam and arrange the sliced strawberries in concentric circles over the mousse. If necessary, reheat the strawberry jam and glaze the strawberries lightly.

7 Chill the tart in the refrigerator for about 3–4 hours, or until the chocolate mousse has set. Cut into slices and serve.

3

4

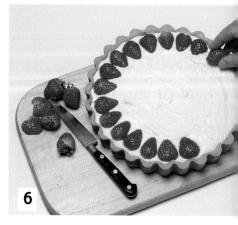
6

Chocolate Profiteroles

INGREDIENTS

Serves 4

For the pastry:

150 ml/¼ pint water
50 g/2 oz butter
65 g/2½ oz plain flour, sifted
2 medium eggs, lightly beaten

For the custard:

300 ml/½ pint milk
pinch of freshly grated nutmeg
3 medium egg yolks
50 g/2 oz caster sugar
2 tbsp plain flour, sifted
2 tbsp cornflour, sifted

For the sauce:

175 g/6 oz soft brown sugar
150 ml/¼ pint boiling water
1 tsp instant coffee
1 tbsp cocoa powder
1 tbsp brandy
75 g/3 oz butter
1 tbsp golden syrup

1 Preheat the oven to 220°C/425°F/Gas Mark 7, 15 minutes before cooking. Lightly oil two baking sheets. For the pastry, place the water and the butter in a heavy-based saucepan and bring to the boil. Remove from the heat and beat in the flour. Return to the heat and cook for 1 minute or until the mixture forms a ball in the centre of the saucepan.

2 Remove from the heat and leave to cool slightly, then gradually beat in the eggs a little at a time, beating well after each addition. Once all the eggs have been added, beat until the paste is smooth and glossy. Pipe or spoon 20 small balls onto the baking sheets, allowing plenty of room for expansion.

3 Bake in the preheated oven for 25 minutes or until well risen and golden brown. Reduce the oven temperature to 180°C/350°F/Gas Mark 4. Make a hole in each ball and continue to bake for a further 5 minutes. Remove from the oven and leave to cool.

4 For the custard, place the milk and nutmeg in a heavy-based saucepan and bring to the boil. In another saucepan, whisk together the egg yolks, sugar and the flours, then beat in the hot milk. Bring to the boil and simmer, whisking constantly for 2 minutes. Cover and leave to cool.

5 Spoon the custard into the profiteroles and arrange on a large serving dish. Place all the sauce ingredients in a small saucepan and bring to the boil, then simmer for 10 minutes. Remove from the heat and cool slightly before serving with the chocolate profiteroles.

1

2

5

Iced Chocolate & Raspberry Mousse

INGREDIENTS

Serves 4

12 sponge finger biscuits
juice of 2 oranges
2 tbsp Grand Marnier
300 ml/½ pint double cream
175 g/6 oz plain dark chocolate,
   broken into small pieces
225 g/8 oz frozen raspberries
6 tbsp icing sugar, sifted
cocoa powder, for dusting

To decorate:

few fresh whole raspberries
few mint leaves
grated white chocolate

1 Break the sponge finger biscuits into small pieces and divide between four individual glass dishes. Blend together the orange juice and Grand Marnier, then drizzle evenly over the sponge fingers. Cover with clingfilm and chill in the refrigerator for 30 minutes.

2 Meanwhile, place the cream in a small heavy-based saucepan and heat gently, stirring occasionally until boiling. Remove the saucepan from the heat then add the pieces of dark chocolate and leave to stand, untouched for about 7 minutes. Using a whisk, whisk the chocolate and cream together, until the chocolate has melted and is well blended and completely smooth. Leave to cool slightly.

3 Place the frozen raspberries and icing sugar into a food processor or liquidizer and blend until roughly crushed.

4 Fold the crushed raspberries into the cream and chocolate mixture and mix lightly until well blended. Spoon over the chilled sponge finger biscuits. Lightly dust with a little cocoa powder and decorate with whole raspberries, mint leaves and grated white chocolate. Serve immediately.

HELPFUL HINT

Remove the raspberries from the freezer about 20 minutes before you need to purée them. This will soften them slightly but they will still be frozen.

Chocolate Raspberry Mille Feuille

INGREDIENTS

Serves 6

450 g/1 lb puff pastry,
   thawed if frozen
1 quantity Raspberry Chocolate
   Ganache (*see* page 24), chilled
700 g/1½ lbs fresh raspberries, plus
   extra for decorating
icing sugar for dusting

For the raspberry sauce:
225 g/8 oz fresh raspberries
2 tbsp seedless raspberry jam
1–2 tbsp caster sugar, or to taste
2 tbsp lemon juice or
   framboise liqueur

HELPFUL HINT

If you prefer, make one big mille feuille by leaving the three strips whole in step 2. Slice the finished mille feuille with a sharp serrated knife.

1 Preheat the oven to 200°C/400°F/Gas Mark 6, 15 minutes before baking. Lightly oil a large baking sheet and sprinkle with a little water. Roll out the pastry on a lightly floured surface to a rectangle about 43 x 28 cm/17 x 11 inches. Cut into three long strips. Mark each strip crossways at 6.5 cm/2½ inch intervals using a sharp knife; this will make cutting the baked pastry easier and neater. Carefully transfer to the baking sheet, keeping the edges as straight as possible.

2 Bake in the preheated oven for 20 minutes or until well risen and golden brown. Place on a wire rack and leave to cool. Carefully transfer each rectangle to a work surface and using a sharp knife, trim the long edges straight. Cut along the knife marks to make 18 rectangles.

3 Place all the ingredients for the raspberry sauce in a food processor and blend until smooth. If the purée is too thick, add a little water. Taste and adjust the sweetness if necessary. Strain into a bowl, cover and chill in the refrigerator.

4 Place one pastry rectangle on the work surface flat-side down, spread with a little chocolate ganache and sprinkle with a few fresh raspberries. Spread a second rectangle with a little ganache, place over the first, pressing gently, then sprinkle with a few raspberries. Place a third rectangle on top, flat-side up, and spread with a little chocolate ganache.

5 Arrange some raspberries on top and dust lightly with a little icing sugar. Repeat with the remaining pastry rectangles, chocolate ganache and fresh raspberries.

6 Chill in the refrigerator until required and serve with the raspberry sauce and any remaining fresh raspberries.

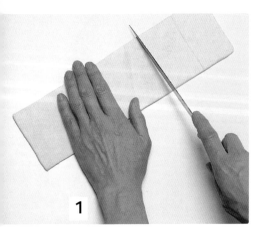

1

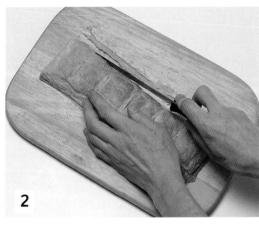

2

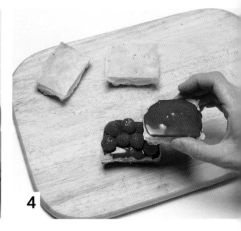

4

Vanilla & Lemon Panna Cotta with Raspberry Sauce

INGREDIENTS

Serves 6

900 ml/1½ pints double cream
1 vanilla pod, split
100 g/3½ oz caster sugar
zest of 1 lemon
3 sheets gelatine
5 tbsp milk
450 g/1 lb raspberries
3–4 tbsp icing sugar, to taste
1 tbsp lemon juice
extra lemon zest, to decorate

1 Put the cream, vanilla pod and sugar into a saucepan. Bring to the boil, then simmer for 10 minutes until slightly reduced, stirring to prevent scalding. Remove from the heat, stir in the lemon zest and remove the vanilla pod.

2 Soak the gelatine in the milk for 5 minutes, or until softened. Squeeze out any excess milk and add to the hot cream. Stir well until dissolved.

3 Pour the cream mixture into six ramekins or mini pudding moulds and leave in the refrigerator for 4 hours, or until set.

4 Meanwhile, put 175 g/6 oz of the raspberries in a food processor with the icing sugar and lemon juice. Blend to a purée then pass the mixture through a sieve. Fold in the remaining raspberries with a metal spoon or rubber spatula and chill in the refrigerator until ready to serve.

5 To serve, dip each of the moulds into hot water for a few seconds, then turn out on to six individual serving plates. Spoon some of the raspberry sauce over and around the panna cotta, decorate with extra lemon zest and serve.

TASTY TIP

Sheet gelatine is readily available from large supermarkets. It is much easier to measure and use than powdered gelatine and also gives a glossier finish to clear jellies.

Bomba Siciliana

INGREDIENTS

Serves 6–8

100 g/3½ oz plain chocolate, broken
   into pieces
200 g/7 oz fresh chilled custard
150 ml/¼ pint whipping cream
25 g/1 oz candied peel,
   finely chopped
25 g/1 oz glacé cherries, chopped
25 g/1 oz sultanas
3 tbsp rum
225 g/8 oz good-quality vanilla
   ice cream
200 ml/¼ pint double cream
3 tbsp caster sugar

1 Melt the plain chocolate in bowl set over a saucepan of simmering water until smooth, then cool. Whisk together the custard with the whipping cream and slightly cooled chocolate. Spoon the mixture into a shallow, lidded freezer box and freeze. Every 2 hours, remove from the freezer and using an electric whisk or balloon whisk, whisk thoroughly. Repeat 3 times, then leave until frozen solid. Soak the candied peel, cherries and sultanas in the rum and leave until needed.

2 Chill a bombe or 1 litre/1¾ pint pudding mould in the freezer for about 30 minutes. Remove the chocolate ice cream from the freezer to soften, then spoon the ice cream into the mould and press down well, smoothing around the edges and leaving a hollow in the centre. Return the ice cream to the freezer for about 1 hour, or until frozen hard.

3 Remove the vanilla ice cream from the freezer to soften. Spoon the softened vanilla ice cream into the hollow, making sure to leave another hollow for the cream. Return to the freezer again and freeze until hard.

4 Whip the cream and sugar until it is just holding its shape then fold in the soaked fruit. Remove the mould from the freezer and spoon in the cream mixture. Return to the freezer for at least another hour.

5 When ready to serve, remove the mould from the freezer and dip into hot water for a few seconds, then turn on to a large serving plate. Dip a knife into hot water and cut into wedges to serve.

TASTY TIP

For the best flavour, buy whole candied peel. Cut it into strips using kitchen scissors, then chop crosswise into small pieces.

1

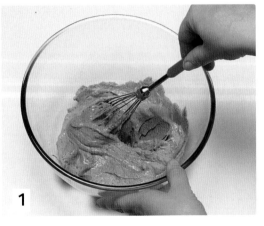

1

2

Tiramisu

INGREDIENTS

Serves 4

225 g/8 oz mascarpone cheese
25 g/1 oz icing sugar, sifted
150 ml/¼ pint strong brewed
   coffee, chilled
300 ml/½ pint double cream
3 tbsp coffee liqueur
125 g/4 oz Savoiardi or
   sponge finger biscuits
50 g/2 oz plain dark chocolate, grated
   or made into small curls
cocoa powder, for dusting
assorted summer berries, to serve

1 Lightly oil and line a 900 g/2 lb loaf tin with a piece of clingfilm. Put the mascarpone cheese and icing sugar into a large bowl and using a rubber spatula, beat until smooth. Stir in 2 tablespoons of chilled coffee and mix thoroughly.

2 Whip the cream with 1 tablespoon of the coffee liqueur until just thickened. Stir a spoonful of the whipped cream into the mascarpone mixture, then fold in the rest. Spoon half of the the mascarpone mixture into the prepared loaf tin and smooth the top.

3 Put the remaining coffee and coffee liqueur into a shallow dish just bigger than the biscuits. Using half of the biscuits, dip one side of each biscuit into the coffee mixture, then arrange on top of the mascarpone mixture in a single layer. Spoon the rest of the mascarpone mixture over the biscuits and smooth the top.

4 Dip the remaining biscuits in the coffee mixture and arrange on top of the mascarpone mixture. Drizzle with any remaining coffee mixture. Cover with clingfilm and chill in the refrigerator for 4 hours.

5 Carefully turn the tiramisu out on to a large serving plate and sprinkle with the grated chocolate or chocolate curls. Dust with cocoa powder, cut into slices and serve with a few summer berries.

FOOD FACT

This now classic Italian dessert appears in all kinds of forms in most Italian cookery books. The name literally means 'pick me up'.

1

2

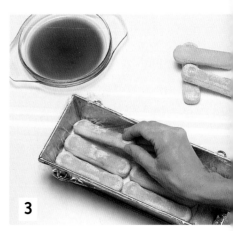

3

Chocolate & Rum Truffles

INGREDIENTS

Makes 44

For the chocolate truffles:

225 g/8 oz plain chocolate
25 g/1 oz butter, softened
2 medium egg yolks
2 tsp brandy or kirsch
2 tsp double cream
24 maraschino cherries, drained
2 tbsp cocoa powder, sifted

For the rum truffles:

125 g/4 oz plain dark chocolate
2 tbsp rum
125 ml/4 fl oz double cream
50 g/2 oz ground almonds
2 tbsp icing sugar, sifted

TASTY TIP

These truffles are so easy to make, they are great to give as gifts. Roll some in icing sugar, as above, and roll others in cocoa powder. Arrange in a gift box in a chequerboard pattern.

1 For the chocolate truffles, break the chocolate into pieces and place in a heatproof bowl set over a saucepan of gently simmering water. Leave for 20 minutes or until the chocolate has melted. Stir until the chocolate is smooth and remove from the heat. Leave to stand for about 6 minutes.

2 Beat the butter, the egg yolks, the brandy or kirsch and double cream together until smooth. Stir the melted chocolate into the butter and egg yolk mixture and stir until thick. Cover and leave to cool for about 30 minutes. Chill in the refrigerator for 1 ½ hours or until firm.

3 Divide the truffle mixture into 24 pieces and mould around the drained cherries. Roll in the cocoa powder until evenly coated. Place the truffles in petit four paper cases and chill in the refrigerator for 2 hours before serving.

4 To make the rum truffles, break the chocolate into small pieces and place in a heavy-based saucepan with the cream and rum. Heat gently until the chocolate has melted, then stir until smooth. Stir in the ground almonds and pour into a small bowl and chill in the refrigerator for at least 6 hours or until the mixture is thick.

5 Remove the truffle from the refrigerator and shape small spoonfuls, about the size of a cherry, into balls. Roll in the sifted icing sugar and place in petit four paper cases. Store the truffles in the refrigerator until ready to serve.

1

2

3

Shortbread Thumbs

INGREDIENTS

Makes 12

125 g/4 oz self-raising flour
125 g/4 oz butter, softened
25 g/1 oz white vegetable fat
50 g/2 oz granulated sugar
25 g/1 oz cornflour, sifted
5 tbsp cocoa powder, sifted
125 g/4 oz icing sugar
6 assorted coloured glacé cherries,
  rinsed, dried and halved

FOOD FACT

Using a combination of butter and vegetable fat gives these biscuits a softer texture than using all butter.

HELPFUL HINT

After baking, remove the cooked biscuits as soon as possible from the baking sheets as they will continue to cook and could overcook. Cool completely on wire cooling racks before storing in airtight tins.

1 Preheat the oven to 150°C/300°F/Gas Mark 2, 10 minutes before baking. Lightly oil two baking sheets. Sift the flour into a large bowl, cut 75 g/3 oz of the butter and the white vegetable fat into small cubes, add to the flour, then, using your fingertips, rub in until the mixture resembles fine breadcrumbs.

2 Stir in the granulated sugar, sifted cornflour and 4 tablespoons of cocoa powder and bring the mixture together with your hand to form a soft and pliable dough.

3 Place on a lightly floured surface and shape into 12 small balls. Place onto the baking sheets at least 5 cm/2 inches apart, then press each one with a clean thumb to make a dent.

4 Bake in the preheated oven for 20–25 minutes. Remove from the oven and leave for 1–2 minutes to cool. Transfer to a wire rack and leave until cold.

5 Sift the icing sugar and the remaining cocoa powder into a bowl and add the remaining softened butter. Blend to form a smooth and spreadable icing with 1–2 tablespoons of hot water. Spread a little icing over the top of each biscuit and place half a cherry on each. Leave until set before serving.

1

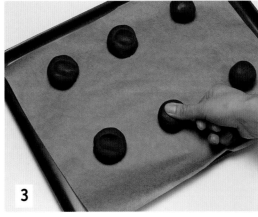
3

5

Chocolate Orange Biscuits

INGREDIENTS

Makes 30

100 g/3½ oz plain dark chocolate
125 g/4 oz butter
125 g/4 oz caster sugar
pinch of salt
1 medium egg, beaten
grated zest of 2 oranges
200 g/7 oz plain flour
1 tsp baking powder
125 g/4 oz icing sugar
1–2 tbsp orange juice

HELPFUL HINT

To get the maximum amount of juice from citrus fruits, heat the whole fruit in the microwave for about 40 seconds, then cool slightly before squeezing. Alternatively, roll the fruit on the table, pressing lightly before squeezing out the juice. It is important to add the orange juice gradually to the icing mixture because you may not need all of it to obtain a spreadable consistency.

1 Preheat the oven to 200°C/400°F/Gas Mark 6, 15 minutes before baking. Lightly oil several baking sheets. Coarsely grate the chocolate and reserve. Beat the butter and sugar together until creamy. Add the salt, beaten egg and half the orange zest and beat again.

2 Sift the flour and baking powder, add to the bowl with the grated chocolate and beat to form a dough. Shape into a ball, wrap in clingfilm and chill in the refrigerator for 2 hours.

3 Roll the dough out on a lightly floured surface to 5 mm/¼ inch thickness and cut into 5 cm/2 inch rounds. Place the rounds on the prepared baking sheets, allowing room for expansion. Bake in the preheated oven for 10–12 minutes or until firm. Remove the biscuits from the oven and leave to cool slightly. Using a spatula, transfer to a wire rack and leave to cool.

4 Sift the icing sugar into a small bowl and stir in sufficient orange juice to make a smooth, spreadable icing. Pipe spirals of icing on to the biscuits, leave until almost set, then sprinkle on the remaining grated orange zest before serving.

1

2

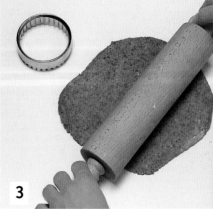

3

Rich Chocolate Cup Cakes

INGREDIENTS

Makes 12

175 g/6 oz self-raising flour
25 g/1 oz cocoa powder
175 g/6 oz soft light brown sugar
75 g/3 oz butter, melted
2 medium eggs, lightly beaten
1 tsp vanilla essence
40 g/1½ oz maraschino cherries,
    drained and chopped

For the chocolate icing:
50 g/2 oz plain dark chocolate
25 g/1 oz unsalted butter
25 g/1 oz icing sugar, sifted

For the cherry icing:
125 g/4 oz icing sugar
7 g/¼ oz unsalted butter, melted
1 tsp syrup from the
    maraschino cherries
3 maraschino cherries, halved,
    to decorate

1. Preheat the oven to 180°C/350°F/Gas Mark 4, 10 minutes before baking. Line a 12 hole muffin or deep bun tin tray with paper muffin cases. Sift the flour and cocoa powder into a bowl. Stir in the sugar, then add the melted butter, eggs and vanilla essence. Beat together with a wooden spoon for 3 minutes or until well blended.

2. Divide half the mixture between six of the paper cases. Dry the cherries thoroughly on absorbent kitchen paper, then fold into the remaining mixture and spoon into the rest of the paper cases.

3. Bake on the shelf above the centre of the preheated oven for 20 minutes, or until a skewer inserted into the centre of a cake comes out clean. Transfer to a wire rack and leave to cool.

4. For the chocolate icing, melt the chocolate and butter in a heatproof bowl set over a saucepan of hot water. Remove from the heat and leave to cool for 3 minutes, stirring occasionally. Stir in the icing sugar. Spoon over the six plain chocolate cakes and leave to set.

5. For the cherry icing, sift the icing sugar into a bowl and stir in 1 tablespoon of boiling water, the butter and cherry syrup. Spoon the icing over the remaining six cakes, decorate each with a halved cherry and leave to set.

Step-by-Step, Practical Recipes Party Food: Tips & Hints

Helpful Hint

Frying in oil that is not hot enough causes food to absorb more oil than it would if fried at the correct temperature. If you do not have a thermometer, it is still possible to test the temperature. Drop a cube of bread into the frying pan. If the bread browns in 30 seconds the oil is at the right temperature. If it does not, try again in a couple of minutes or increase the heat. If the bread goes very dark, decrease the heat and add about 150 ml/½ pint of cold oil and test again.

Helpful Hint

When cooking, be particularly careful to keep cooked and raw food separate to avoid any contamination. It is worth washing all fruits and vegetables regardless of whether they are going to be eaten raw or lightly cooked. This rule should apply even to prewashed herbs and salads. Do not reheat food more than once.

Helpful Hint

Decide what kind of entertaining you wish to do, as there are many types of parties: dinner parties, barbecues, picnics, cheese and wine events and even a disco. The type of party will dictate the type of food and how formal it will be.

Tasty Tip

To add decoration to some of your dishes, you can add spring onion curls. To make a spring onion curl, trim off the root and some green top to leave 10 cm/4 inches. Make a 3 cm/1¼ inch cut down from the top, then make another cut at a right angle to the first cut. Continue making fine cuts. Soak the spring onions in iced water for 20 minutes and they open up and curl.

Helpful Hint

When choosing wine for a party, you should choose ones which are of medium price. Cheap wines taste cheap and your guests will not be impressed; expensive wines, on the other hand, will most probably not be appreciated in the general chat and movement.

Helpful Hint

The best foods when planning a barbecue are steak, chicken pieces, and sausages, small whole fish such as sardines, all of which can be cooked whole or cut into cubes and skewed for kebabs. When barbecuing, it is vital that the food is cooked properly. Semi-cooked sausages and chicken are one of the main causes of stomach upsets.

Helpful Hint

If you are making individual puddings, look for individual plastic pudding basins to cook them in. They are very easy to unmould, as you simply squeeze them to release the pudding.

Helpful Hint

To make life easier and the party less stressful, work out a time plan early on. This will enable you to cook ahead if possible, thus saving time and effort on the day. If you are trying a new recipe, it is also a good idea to cook it beforehand to ensure that it works and tastes good.

Food Fact

Meat, poultry, fish, seafood and dairy products should all be refrigerated. The temperature of the refrigerator should be between 1–5°C/34–41°F, while the freezer temperature should not rise above -18°C/-0.4°F.

Food Fact

Chocolate is available in many different forms from cocoa powder to couveture, which is the best chocolate to use for cooking as it has a high cocoa butter content and melts very smoothly.

Food Fact

Tiramisu is a particularly popular dessert when entertaining. The name literally means 'pick me up'.

Helpful Hint

When hosting a drinks party, it is a good idea to serve some light starters, as this will help to offset too many alcoholic drinks. It is a good idea to offer at least four or five different snacks, with at least two vegetarian choices. Drinks can be kept simple with the offer of red or white wine and beer with plenty of soft drinks. Warm punch in the winter and Pimms in the summer are both excellent choices.

First published in 2013 by
FLAME TREE PUBLISHING LTD
Crabtree Hall, Crabtree Lane, Fulham,
London, SW6 6TY, United Kingdom
www.flametreepublishing.com

NOTE: Recipes using uncooked eggs should be avoided by infants, the elderly, pregnant women and anyone suffering from an illness.

18 17 16 15 14 13   10 9 8 7 6 5 4 3 2 1

ISBN: 978-0-85775-862-0

ACKNOWLEDGEMENTS: Authors: Catherine Atkinson, Juliet Barker, Gina Steer, Vicki Smallwood, Carol Tennant, Mari Mererid Williams, Elizabeth Wolf-Cohen and Simone Wright. Photography: Colin Bowling, Paul Forrester and Stephen Brayne. Home Economists and Stylists: Jacqueline Bellefontaine, Mandy Phipps, Vicki Smallwood and Penny Stephens. Some props supplied by Barbara Stewart at Surfaces. Publisher and Creative Director: Nick Wells. Editorial: Catherine Taylor, Laura Bulbeck, Esme Chapman, Emma Chafer, Gina Steer and Karen Fitzpatrick. Design and Production: Chris Herbert, Mike Spender and Helen Wall.